Th
LITTLE BOOK
of
CELTIC BLESSINGS

by
Iain Tweedale

Published 2021 by Guided Pilgrimage, Brynseion, Cwrtnewydd, Llanybydder, Ceredigion, Cymru SA40 9YJ
www.guidedpilgrimage.co.uk

ISBN 978-1-7398523-0-6

Designed by Christine Smith, Guided Pilgrimage

CONTENTS

INTRODUCTION

These blessings speak to the heart in times of uncertainty and show that there is love, light and hope for us all.

They help us to take a little time out of our busy lives to discover the old rhythms of life that can still be seen in the Celtic lands of Ireland, Scotland and Wales.

Through them we may experience that we are part of something bigger than just ourselves and they might even give us a glimpse of a connection with this wider reality as we walk together through these beautiful, wild Celtic landscapes.

I hope you enjoy them.
Iain

Iain Tweedale lives in the far west of Wales overlooking the Irish Sea. He is a lay Cistercian connected to Caldey Abbey and loves to share wild Celtic landscapes with visitors who come on his pilgrimages and guided holidays with Guided Pilgrimage, Waterford Camino Tours and Journeying:

www.guidedpilgrimage.co.uk
www.waterfordcamino.com
www.journeying.co.uk

1. TIME

May you experience time the old way,
As a friend rather than the enemy,
As a bringer of joy,
Not a bringer of deadlines.
May it loop around you,
And enfold you with possibilities.
May it embrace you with love.

St Declan's Cathedral,
Ardmore, Co Waterford

2. SLOW & SENSE

May you slow and sense the landscape around you,
To hear the waves and watch for the tide,
To feel the breath of warm breeze on your face,
To hear the wind alive high in the trees above,
To taste the salt of the sea on your lips,
To feel the water from the stream,
Run between your fingers,
May you slow and sense unity,
With the landscape around you.

3. THE WORLD ANEW

May your journey bring new sights,
To see the world anew.
May your journey bring new sounds,
To hear the world anew.
May your journey bring new wonder,
To feel a joy anew.
And may your journey bring new love,
To start a life anew.

St David's Way, Pembrokeshire

St Non's Chapel, Pembrokeshire

4. FORGIVENESS

May the sunrise show you how to see clearly,
To start again,
To forgive yourself and others,
To learn to let go,
To recover yourself,
To renew yourself,
At the start of this beautiful new day.

5. PRAYER FROM THE MONASTERY

In the stillness of the night Vigil,
I will pray for you.
With the coming light at Lauds,
I will pray for you.
In the pause from work at Sext,
I will pray for you.
In the afternoon's heat at None,
I will pray for you.
As work ends with Vespers,
I will pray for you.
As night brings silence after Compline,
I will pray for you.
May my prayers around this day,
Bring love, hope and peace to you.

6. RHYTHM

May you find a new rhythm,
To have time to hear and listen,
To see and to understand,
To pause for a story or a song.
May this new rhythm connect and protect you,
To find a new way to belong.

7. FRIENDS

May you make good friends,
Who know and love you,
Who accept your flaws and fears.
Friends to share your laughter,
And friends to dry your tears.
May they be there when you need them.
May they tell you when you hurt them.
May you celebrate and mourn with them,
And may you always walk beside them.

8. BEING YOURSELF

May you learn to be yourself,
To be happy in your skin,
To know where you are going,
And learn from where you've been.
May your guide show you the true path.
May your feet find solid ground.
May your journey be eventful,
And your way home be finally found.

9. WHEN THE SEA AND SKY MERGE

When sea and sky merge,
May you find beauty and being.
With wave and tide's speed,
May you find a new way of seeing.
Through silence and prayer,
May you find a new life for living.

LOOKING OVER THE IRISH SEA TO IRELAND

10. HEAVEN

Through the breaking of the waves,
May you hear heaven.
Through the stars in clear night skies,
May you see heaven.
Through myriad grains of sand,
May you touch heaven.
Through sweet crystal springwater,
May you taste heaven.
Through all your senses,
May you know heaven, now.

11. A BLESSING FOR THIS DAY

May you be blessed,
With love this morning.
May you be blessed,
With hope this afternoon.
May you be blessed,
With kindness this evening.
And may you be blessed
With peace this night.

12. THE WAY

May the way show you the truth,
The truth about love and the cost of loving all.
May the way show you the truth about forgiveness,
For your sake, not just the sake of the forgiven.
May the way show you the truth about judging,
That we are in no position to judge.
May the way show you the truth about trust,
That we do not have to be in control.
And may the way show you the truth about life,
That the journey is itself the destination.

13. LIGHT

May your light shine out,
To reach those at sea who have lost their way.
May your light shine out,
To reach those at sea without hope.
May your light shine out,
To reach those drifting towards hidden rocks.
May your light shine out,
To guide us to the safe haven of your love.

14. JUST ASK

If you are anxious,
Just ask and I will hear.
If you are suffering,
Just ask and I will draw near.
If you are in pain,
Just ask and I will hear.
If you feel overwhelmed,
Just ask and I will draw near.

15. PATIENCE

If a mist descends to obscure the way,
With time it will become clear.
If the path is overgrown today,
With time it will re-appear.
If the tide is too low to make sail,
With time it will float you clear.
And if you put your trust in me,
With time you will lose your fear.

St David's Shrine, St David's Cathedral

16. LITTLE THINGS

In the little things you will find me,
In the cleaning and the washing,
In the shopping and the gardening,
In a kind word or simple favour,
In a conversation and in laughter.
In these little things you will find me.

17. FINDING YOUR WAY

If the path ahead has reached a fork,
Pause awhile where we can talk.
If there is no easy choice,
Talk to me, I know your voice.
I will listen to all your fears,
And the right way will become crystal clear.

St Ann's Head, Pembrokeshire

18. INVITATION

Come and see,
And you may find,
The way to unlock,
Your peace of mind.
Come and see,
And you may find,
Light, love and hope,
For all humankind.
Come and see,
And you may find,
How to open your eyes,
And be no longer blind.

19. GLENDALOUGH

May the silence of the lough,
Speak to you.
And the boughs of the trees,
Shelter you.
May the prayers of the saints,
Enfold you.
And the safety of the stones,
Protect you,
With the silence of the lough.

RIVER TEIFI, CEREDIGION AND CARMARTHENSHIRE

20. PROMISES

Know that I am with you always,
Through life's highs and lows.
Know that I will listen always,
Your inner thoughts you can show.
Know that we are beginners always,
Together we will learn and grow.

21. UNITY

May the sea take you to find new places.
May the land bring you home to kind faces.
May the wind carry words of love and simplicity.
May the stars show you the wonders of infinity,
And may your soul experience peace through unity.

Sgwd yr Eira Waterfall,
Brecon Beacons

22. TAKING TIME

Take this time,
To journey around yourself,
And discover who you truly are.
Take this time,
To consider changes facing you,
And find a new way to be.
Take this time,
To connect with something bigger,
And experience a new reality.

23. CONNECTION

May the warm sun soften all tenseness,
And open your heart to those around you.
May the deep ocean bring cool waters,
To calm you in heated times.
May the rich earth bring the fruits of the land,
To sustain and nourish you.
May you feel connected and united,
In love and at peace.

24. LISTENING

May you learn how to listen,
To the message of the wind in the trees,
And the breaking wave on the shore,
To connect you to the world around you.
May you learn how to listen,
To the message of the least in the room,
And hear what you need to know,
To receive wisdom from those around you.

25. BELONGING

May you know that you are loved and needed.
May you know that you are cared for and wanted.
May you know that your feelings matter,
And are heeded
May you know that you belong,
And to you I will always be committed.

26. FIND YOURSELF

May you find yourself,
Through love.
May you find yourself,
Through kindness.
May you find yourself,
Through listening.
May you find yourself,
Through simple things,
And may you find yourself at peace.

27. BE STILL

Be still and know the meaning,
Of the beauty of the mountain.
Be still and know the meaning,
Of the river flowing to the sea.
Be still and know the meaning,
In the silence of the forest.
Be still and know the meaning
Of the divine.

28. SEARCHING

If you are searching for belief,
That cannot easily be found,
May you see God in love,
in light and goodness.
That is where God will be found.

29. LOVE

If you are searching for the answer,
May you find that it is simple,
The answer is love.
Not words and intellect,
The answer is love.
Not money and possessions,
The answer is love.
Not status and position,
The answer is love.
Not expectations and judgement,
May you find that it is simple, just love.

30. TAKE TIME TO STOP

Take time to stop,
And see what you did not see before.
Take time to stop,
And hear what you did not hear before.
Take time to stop,
And talk how you did not talk before.
Take time to stop,
And love in a way you did not love before.
Take time to stop,
And live in a way you did not live before.

31. SEASONS

May you learn from the seasons around you,
The subtle changes in life without and within.
May bud and blossom bear rich harvest,
As leaves turn from green to gold.
May the passion of youth learn wisdom,
As you take time to listen to elders.
May short days yield stories of ancestors,
As you gather with friends around the fire.
May you learn that there is a season for everything.

32. CLIFF TOPS

Today I walked on a cliff top to St Davids,
When something caught my eye.
A chough floated effortlessly by,
Suspended by the breeze riding up the cliffs.
Its unmistakable call sounded as if to say:
May the divine wind hold you safe and high.
May you find time to stop a while and see,
That you are blessed to be part of all this.

MARLOES, PEMBROKESHIRE

33. THE PERSON IN FRONT OF YOU

May you see the person in front of you,
Just for what they need.
May you learn how to ask what you can do,
To help them to be freed.
May you see that life is simple,
When you can help to meet their need.

34. PASSING

My friend David died too young last month.
He had a rich and complex journey through life.
Like him may we come to understand,
The essence of humanity,
Through its losses and its joys.
Like him may we ask,
Searching questions of ourselves,
And challenge those around us.
Like him may we find God,
In the most unexpected moments.
Like him may we find peace,
Instead of bitterness at time cut short.
And like his namesake may we find,
The answer to the mystery,
Lies in love and the little things of life.

DINEFWR CASTLE, CARMARTHENSHIRE

TINTERN ABBEY, MONMOUTHSHIRE

35. TINTERN ABBEY

In the hills high above Tintern Abbey,
May you look down,
Invited through the poet's words to imagine nature,
With a quality beyond just beauty.
May you be transported,
By the meandering river to earlier times,
When Cistercian monks and Enlightenment Romantics,
Each in their day,
Saw something more in this sacred land:
Something revealed in a hope of unity.

36 MOUNTAINS

May the mountain be a thin place for you,
Where heaven and earth are near.
May your climb be short,
And may the right path become clear,
As the obscuring mists roll away,
To reveal a new perspective on this beautiful day.

37. ST PATRICK

Today we climbed an ancient hill,
Past the place where Patrick lived,
Before sailing again for Éirinn.
Upwards and still higher we climbed,
Past the tomb of a king written of by Ptolemy,
From lush paths to bare volcanic rock,
And at the summit the wind carried,
Our thoughts of choices to be made.
May you climb to your own summit,
And may your thoughts there be clear.
May you see the path laid out before you
And may you know God is near.

38. BEING IN THE NOW

May the rhythm,
Of your breath,
Your step,
Your prayer,
Bring you to the now.
May the rhythm,
Of the wave,
The tide,
The stream,
Bring you to the now.
May these rhythms,
Connect and unify you,
With the eternity,
Of being in the now.

39. OCEAN

The water of the ocean is eternal.
Waves and tide return again and again,
Gently and sometimes with force,
To soften and shape even hearts of rock.
May the water of the spirit,
Shape you and form you,
Into being the person you long to be.

BOAT TRIP TO SKOMER ISLAND, PEMBROKESHIRE

40. NINE WELLS

May you let your emotions flow,
Like water from the well.
May you let your dreams flow,
Like water from the well.
May your sufferings run away,
Like water from the well.
May you be moved from deep within,
Like water from the well.
May your heart be gently softened,
By the water from the well.
May your fears be washed away,
By the water from the well.
May entanglements unravel,
With water from the well.
May your imagination be inspired,
By the water from the well.
And may your soul's thirst be quenched,
By the water from the well.

NINE WELLS, PEMBROKESHIRE

41. WALKING THE WAY

May you find a new rhythm,
Watching the waves,
Listening to the birds,
By walking the Way.
May you find a new rhythm,
Engaging with thoughts,
Conversing with strangers,
By walking the Way.
May you find a new rhythm,
In opening your heart,
And freeing your soul,
By walking the Way.

CAIRN AT CAHIR, CO. TIPPERARY

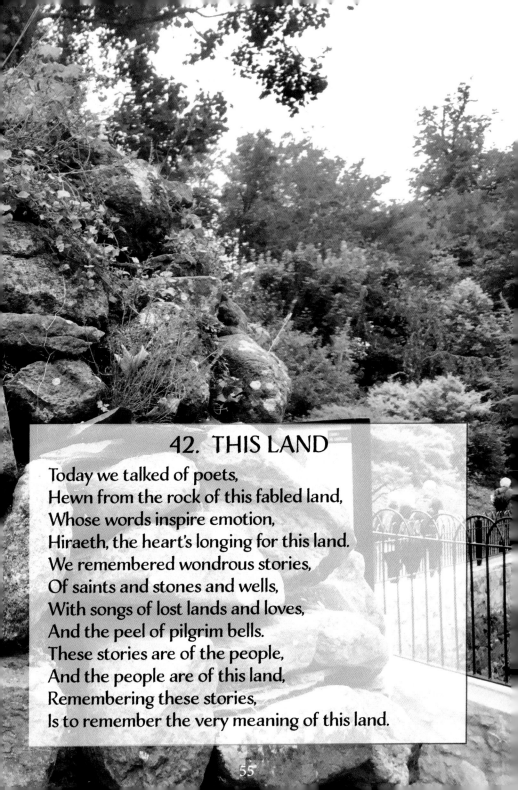

42. THIS LAND

Today we talked of poets,
Hewn from the rock of this fabled land,
Whose words inspire emotion,
Hiraeth, the heart's longing for this land.
We remembered wondrous stories,
Of saints and stones and wells,
With songs of lost lands and loves,
And the peel of pilgrim bells.
These stories are of the people,
And the people are of this land,
Remembering these stories,
Is to remember the very meaning of this land.

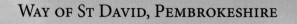

43. ALL WILL BE WELL

Do not worry about the future,
You will survive and prosper,
All will be well,
I am with you always.
Do not worry about past,
Mistakes are forgiven,
All will be well,
I am with you always.
Do not worry about the present,
Be yourself and live for the day,
All will be well,
I am with you always.

44. NIKSEN*

For a little while,
May you have no goals,
Just be.
For a little while,
May you have nothing to do,
Just be.
For a little while,
May you let your mind wander,
Just be.
For a little while,
May you watch the sky and the trees,
Just be.
For a little while,
May you lose all sense of time,
Just be.
For a little while,
May there be no words,
Just be, with me.

*Dutch word for
doing nothing

45. IN TIMES LIKE THESE

In times like these,
May you know that you are not alone.
In times like these,
May you know that you are loved.
In times like these,
May you know that there will be help.
In times like these,
May you find a new simplicity.
In times like these,
May you see the way with a new clarity.
In times like these,
May those around you draw closer.
In times like these,
May you find hope and a new future.

46. LIGHT, LOVE, GOODNESS

May you discover the divine light,
Beaming out the way ahead.
May you discover the divine love,
Living out in heart not head.
May you discover the divine good,
Finding out with no need to be led.

47. THE HOMECOMING

May the rise of the tide,
Bring the boat safely home for you.
May the song of the birds,
Sound a welcome home for you.
May the fire in the hearth,
Warm the home ready for you.
May the laughter of the children,
Show the family's love for you.
And may this homecoming,
Mark no need to leave again for you.

48. AT THE CENTRE

May you learn how to slow,
And calm your racing mind.
May you learn how to rest,
In the presence of the divine.
May you learn how to let go,
Of thoughts that make you blind.
To the love at your very centre,
That you will surely one day find.

49. ROUGH SEAS

When you are on a rough sea,
May it be calmed for you.
When you are in a dark place,
May it be lightened for you.
When your path has been lost,
May it be found again for you.
When the view is obscured by cloud,
May it be cleared for you.
And when you feel alone,
Know I will be there for you.

50. A CHRISTMAS BLESSING

May you know that however quietly,
A bright new dawn has just begun.
May you know that the darkness is over,
A bright new light has finally come.
May you you know that the waiting has ended,
A bright new hope rises with the sun.

51. A NEW YEAR BLESSING

If you look,
May you find,
That love and peace,
Are a state of mind.
To put ourselves,
In the shoes of others,
Will make us into,
Sisters and brothers.

CAHIR, CO. TIPPERARY

SOLVA, PEMBROKESHIRE

52. PEACE

May you see peace,
In the view from the mountain.
May you hear peace,
In the wave breaking on the shore.
May you taste peace,
In the sweet water from the spring.
May you touch peace,
In the lush grass of the meadow.
May the peace of the divine,
Come to dwell in your heart.
Peace.

FOR MORE INFORMATION

If you would like any further information or would like to join us on a Celtic pilgrimage, please get in touch through one of the organisations shown below. We look forward to hearing from you.

 A not-for-profit travel company providing a range of pilgrimage experiences through Celtic landscapes.
www.guidedpilgrimage.co.uk

 Waterford Camino Tours in Ireland gives you a breather from the world, walking in the steps of those who have gone before.
www.waterfordcamino.com

 Journeying takes small groups on guided walking tour holidays in an informal Christian ambience.
www.journeying.co.uk